Here is the Which Way crew that will stand "bayou" as you travel through Louisiana:

I.Q. Sue plans to add to her knowledge of the state when she visits a former famous sugar plantation.

Robomouse is looking forward to rolling along some curvy balconies in the French Quarter.

Squawker has a mouthful of Cajun expressions that he plans to try out on his Which Way friends.

Table of Contents

WHO is heading for the WHICH WAY HALL OF FAME?

WHAT will be in the WHICH WAY MUSEUM?

WHERE will the WHICH WAY SUPERMAX MOVIE be filmed?

"Easy" Does It

You begin your Louisiana adventure in the state's largest city, New Orleans. Known as "The Big Easy," New Orleans is said to be a place where you can leave your worries behind and have fun. This Which Way crew is ready for that! Everyone meets in the city's beautiful Garden District, near the Mississippi River. The river curls around the city in the shape of a new moon. This curve of the river gives New Orleans another of its nicknames, "The Crescent City."

Roxanne Rolls visited New Orleans once before. She is eager to lead the crew on her own special tour of the city. She has made a list of things to do. Find each place on Roxanne's list, in order. Then ease on down to the bottom of page 3.

Roxanne's List

1. Snap a photo of Louis Armstrong's first trumpet at the Jazz Museum.
2. Pet a live shark at the aquarium.
3. Let Robomouse roll around on "Mardi Grass."
4. Ride an old wooden carousel in one of the largest city parks in the U.S.
5. Take a ride on a historic streetcar.
6. Take Squawker to see the sculpture garden at the art museum.
7. Eat dinner on a Mississippi River steamboat.
8. Buy some souvenirs and pastries at an open-air market.

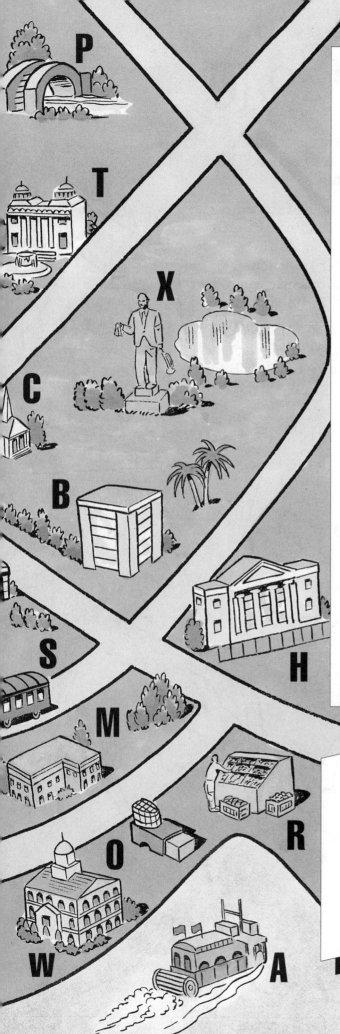

CITY MAP KEY

 Superdome: Home stadium of the New Orleans Saints, who play football on artificial turf called "Mardi Grass"

 Audubon Zoo: A top-rated zoo that is home to 1,500 animals

 French Market: Famous open-air market in the French Quarter

 Audubon Aquarium of the Americas: Features a Caribbean reef tunnel and 400,000-gallon Gulf of Mexico display

 City Park: One of the country's largest city parks

 The Cabildo: Building where the Louisiana Purchase was formalized

 Old U.S. Mint: Former federal mint that now houses the Jazz Museum and the Carnival Museum

 Steamboat *Natchez***:** Restored steamboat that offers jazz and dinner cruises on the Mississippi River

 St. Charles Avenue Streetcar: Famous old streetcar line that is a national historic landmark

 New Orleans Museum of Art: Forty-six galleries of art and sculpture from around the world

Did you visit all the sites on the list? At each location, there is a letter. Write those letters, in the order you found them, in the spaces below:

___ ___ ___ ___ ___ ___ ___ ___
1   2   3   4   5   6   7   8

Use this clue to cross off a famous Pelican Stater on page 28.

Carnival Code

New Orleans is known for its fantastic food, great music, and rich history. It is also famous for its annual Mardi Gras celebration. The Which Way crew arrives just in time to join in the fun.

The gang hurries to Canal Street to catch a parade, one of the daily traditions of this festival. Many people here are dressed in costumes and masks. Wearing colorful masks is another tradition. As the parade floats pass by, Sue tells you about yet another tradition— "throws" and "catches." People on the floats toss out brightly colored Mardi Gras beads and metal coins called doubloons. People in the crowd try to catch as many as they can.

As the crew makes some catches, you can grab a clue. Use the letters you find to crack the code on page 5. Then "float" down to the bottom of the page.

4

Have you "unmasked" the code? Now turn to page 28 and use the information to cross one person off your list.

ALL THAT JAZZ

After the parade is over, the crew is ready for another classic New Orleans experience—live jazz music. The city is known as the birthplace of jazz. The first jazz record was made here in 1917 by the Original Dixieland Jazz Band. Jazz blends the best of many musical styles, including blues, brass-band marches, and classical. Many well-known jazz artists are New Orleans natives, including Louis Armstrong, Jelly Roll Morton, and Wynton Marsalis.

Roxanne wants to go to Preservation Hall. This world-famous spot is a great place to hear bands perform traditional jazz. While everyone enjoys the music, you have some notes of your own to make. Fill in the answers to the questions. Then tune in to the bottom of page 7 to compose your next clue.

1. What does "Mardi Gras" mean?

___ ___ ___   ___ ___ ___ ___ ___ ___ ___
  1   2

2. What type of plant life often covers bald cypress trees in Louisiana bayous?

___ ___ ___ ___ ___ ___ ___   ___ ___ ___ ___
    3   4   5

3. What city is home to the world's oldest continuously operating street railway?

___ ___ ___   ___ ___ ___ ___ ___ ___ ___
      6   7

4. "Cajun" is the shortened name of what Canadian people?

___ ___ ___ ___ ___ ___ ___ ___
    8   9

5. What is the name given to the plantation area between Baton Rouge and New Orleans?

___ ___ ___ ___ ___   ___ ___ ___ ___ ___   ___ ___ ___ ___
10   11   12

6. What is the United States' largest single-plant society?

___ ___ ___ ___ ___ ___ ___   ___ ___ ___ ___
      13   14

___ ___ ___ ___ ___ ___
      15

Don't Forget Your Map!
The answers to all of these questions can be found on the *back* of your Louisiana map.

Did you fill in all of the answers? Some of the letters have numbers under them. Write those letters in the correct spaces below.

___ ___ ___ ___ ___ ___   ___ ___ ___ ___ ___ ___   ___ ___ ___ ___ ___ ,
 5   7   3 12 10 13   2   6 13   7   2 15   13   9 10   4   2

___ ___ ___ ___ ___   ___ ___ ___   ___ ___ ___ ___ ___ ___ .
 8 11   5 14 14   5   1   1   8 12   3   5   2 13

Now follow the clue's instructions.

Terrace Twists

After a good night's sleep, the crew is ready to explore more of the city. Willy wants to take a walking tour of the French Quarter. This eighty-five-block area was the original center of the city. Despite its name, most of the houses here are of Spanish design. A fire destroyed most of French-built New Orleans in 1788. At the time, Spain was ruling the city, so Spanish architecture was used to rebuild it.

The French Quarter has narrow cobblestone streets and beautiful buildings with intricate iron balconies. The crew stops to admire one of these buildings. As Robomouse takes a "robo-coaster" ride up and down some of the curvy ironwork, he spies some hidden objects. The items shown on page 9 are hidden in this scene. Once you have spotted them all, "iron" out your next clue at the bottom of the page.

APPLE

MOON

HEART

PAINTBRUSH

LOLLIPOP

DRUM

Did you find all the hidden objects?
Two of them are hidden twice. Write the
first letter of each of their names here:

____ ____

These letters are the initials of a famous
Louisiana native. Turn to page 28 and
cross that person off the list.

Square Route

Before leaving "The Big Easy," the crew members make one final stop. They head to Jackson Square, the heart of the French Quarter. The area, named for Andrew Jackson, features a large bronze statue of the general who defeated the British in the Battle of New Orleans. The St. Louis Cathedral is also located in this public plaza. This magnificent church is one of the oldest Catholic cathedrals in the country.

Jackson Square is a gathering spot for tourists, sidewalk artists, and street performers. The Which Way crew spreads out to join the fun. Meanwhile, you have work to do. Collect the letters described in the clues. As you do, write them in the numbered spaces at the bottom of page 11 to square up your next piece of information.

CLUES

1. The hot-dog vendor is serving the first letter.
2. The second letter is near a bunch of flowers.
3. The juggler is about to catch the third letter.
4. Squawker has the fourth letter.
5. The fifth letter is on a piece of art.
6. The sixth letter is on a balloon.
7. Robomouse is about to roll into the seventh letter.
8. The eighth letter is on a statue.
9. Look in the saxophone for the ninth letter.
10. The last letter is about to be run over by a skater.

Did you write your 10 letters here?

___ ___ ___ ___ ___ ___ ___ ___ ___ ___
 1   2   3   4   5   6   7   8   9   10

Now write the letter that comes *before* each
of these letters in the alphabet.

___ ___ ___ ___ ___ ___ ___ ___ ___ ___

Turn to page 28 and use this final WHO clue
to eliminate a Louisianan.

Plantation Sensations

It is time to say *au revoir* to the French Quarter and all of New Orleans. Sue and Robomouse board a Mississippi riverboat heading north. The rich farmland along this part of the river is dotted with grand old plantations. Many of these homes offer tours to visitors. Some even let tourists spend the night as guests.

The boat stops at White Castle, the site of Nottoway Plantation. Nottoway is the largest plantation in the South. Built in the 1850s for a wealthy planter, it was a working 7,000-acre sugar plantation. The sixty-four-room mansion had indoor bathrooms, gas lamps, and an intercom system—all rare conveniences in the 1800s!

Sue and Robomouse wait outside for the next tour to begin. This is your chance to locate the plantations, past and present, named in the list below. Circle the names in the grid on page 13. They are hidden up, down, forward, backward, and diagonally. Then go to the bottom of the page to harvest your next clue.

LOUISIANA PLANTATIONS

BLYTHEWOOD
BOCAGE
CATALPA
THE COTTAGE
FROGMORE
GLENCOE
GREENWOOD
LAURA
LIVE OAK
MADEWOOD
MAGNOLIA
MELROSE
MOUNT HOPE
OAKLAWN MANOR
ORMOND
PARLANGE
SAN FRANCISCO
TEZCUCO

M	W	E	G	N	A	L	R	A	P	R	G
O	A	K	L	A	W	N	M	A	N	O	R
U	C	G	E	F	R	O	G	M	O	R	E
N	I	U	N	T	E	U	T	M	H	E	E
T	H	E	C	O	T	T	A	G	E	G	N
H	E	W	O	Z	L	D	P	L	S	A	W
O	O	R	E	D	E	I	L	S	O	C	O
P	S	T	A	W	R	T	A	T	R	O	O
E	D	O	O	W	E	H	T	Y	L	B	D
K	A	O	E	V	I	L	A	W	E	I	T
H	D	N	O	M	R	O	C	T	M	H	E
O	C	S	I	C	N	A	R	F	N	A	S

Did you circle all the plantation names?
Now write the uncircled letters, in order from left to
right and top to bottom, in the spaces below.

__ __ __ __ __ __ __ __ __ __ __ __ __ __

" __ __ __ __ __ __ __ __ __ __ __ __ __."

Turn to page 29 and write this clue on the first line.

It's a Shore Thing

Meanwhile, Roxanne, Willy, and Squawker drive southwest to the Gulf of Mexico. Louisiana's coast extends about 400 miles along the Gulf. But the shore has many inlets, islands, and bays, so there are nearly 8,000 miles of coastline. The state's marsh region is rich with marine life, such as shrimp, blue crabs, and oysters.

Willy wants to visit the Louisiana Universities Marine Consortium. This marine research center is located near Cocodrie. Scientists there study the coastline and its marine life. They also offer workshops for students and other visitors.

Roxanne, Willy, and Squawker climb into a canoe and join a salt marsh exploration tour. Meanwhile, you can coast into another clue. Circle the letter of the correct answer to each of these questions. Then paddle over to the bottom of page 15.

Highlights
WHICH WAY
USA?

STATE MAP

Don't Forget Your Map!
All the information you need to answer these questions is on your map of Louisiana.

1. What town in Louisiana is known as the "Frog Capital of the World"?

   s. Snow   **t. Rayne**   **u. Hale**

2. What is Louisiana's state flower?

   h. magnolia   **i. marigold**
   p. camelia

3. Who won the first Sugar Bowl game held in New Orleans in 1935?

   a. Temple University
   i. Tulane University
   o. Crescent College

4. How low is Louisiana's lowest point?

   c. 5 feet above sea level
   n. sea level
   r. 5 feet below sea level

5. What is the annual crawfish harvest in Louisiana?

> **d. 100 million pounds**
> **e. 500 million pounds**
> **o. 1 million tons**

8. Which of these is *not* a state song of Louisiana?

> **g. "You Are My Sunshine"**
> **n. "Bayou Boogie"**
> **t. "Give Me Louisiana"**

6. Which city has a population closest to 200,000?

> **a. Shreveport**   **b. Baton Rouge**
> **c. New Orleans**

9. Which of these is the name of both a major river and lake in Louisiana?

> **c. Atchafalaya**   **d. Sabine**
> **e. Catahoula**

7. When can about half of the continent's migrating birds be found in Louisiana?

> **a. winter**   **f. spring**
> **r. fall**

Have you answered the questions? Write each of the letters you circled in the spaces below.

" "
___ ___ ___ ___ ___ ___ ___ ___ ___
1   2   3   4   5   6   7   8   9

Now turn to page 29 and write these important clue words on the correct line.

LOUISIANA LANGUAGE

Roxanne picks up the rest of the crew and drives north to Baton Rouge. The name *Baton Rouge* means "red stick" in French. A French explorer named the city for a red pole that separated two Native American hunting grounds. After exploring the Old State Capitol, everyone relaxes on the beautiful building's lawn.

Sue reads from her tour guide. It lists more words, many of them French, that are a unique part of Louisiana's culture. Squawker can't resist trying to say the words. But the Which Way bird is so excited that he squawks out some mistakes. Read the list of Squawker's statements on page 17. Decide how many times the Which Way parrot used a "Louisiana" word incorrectly. Then fly down to the bottom of the page.

Guide to "Louisiana" Words

Beignet (ben yay) a powdered-sugar-covered pastry

Boudin (boo dan) a Cajun sausage made with rice

Creole (kree ohl) a person descended from early French and Spanish settlers

Fais do-do (fay doe doe) a Cajun dance party

Gumbo a hearty Cajun soup

Krewe a group that puts on Mardi Gras dances and parades

Lagniappe (lahn yop) a little something extra

Levee (lehv ee) a dike, or wall, built alongside a river to prevent flooding

Muffaletta (muff a lot a) a large sandwich of Italian meats and olive salad

Pirogue (pea rogue) a Cajun fishing boat

Roux (roo) flour browned in a skillet; the basis of many Cajun foods

Two-Step a traditional Cajun dance, similar to a polka

Vieux Carré (vyuh kah ray) the French name for the French Quarter of New Orleans

Zydeco (zie da ko) a musical style featuring the accordion and the washboard

Squawker's "Statements"

1. Sue was hungry for a sandwich, so she ate a MUFFALETTA.

2. Everyone at the Cajun dance was doing the TWO-STEP.

3. Willy floated down the bayou in a ROUX.

4. The last time I ate a BEIGNET, I got powdered sugar all over my beak!

5. I danced at the BOUDIN for hours.

6. If you want to stop a flood around here, you must build a LEVEE.

7. I got to play the washboard in a cool ZYDECO band.

8. In the GUMBO section of New Orleans, we heard music.

9. If you like stew, you've got to try some PIROGUE.

10. Let's help the KREWE decorate for their Mardi Gras dance.

Muffaletta!

Did you figure out how many times the Which Way parrot squawked incorrectly? Use that information to find the correct clue.

If four statements are incorrect, the words are CIRCLE EVERY.

If five are incorrect, the words are REMOVE SEVEN.

If six are incorrect, the words are SWITCH PLACE.

Now turn to page 29 and write the clue words on the proper line.

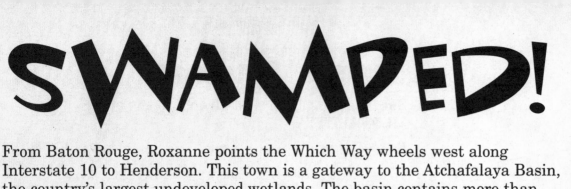

SWAMPED!

From Baton Rouge, Roxanne points the Which Way wheels west along Interstate 10 to Henderson. This town is a gateway to the Atchafalaya Basin, the country's largest undeveloped wetlands. The basin contains more than half a million acres of swamps, lakes, and bayous. It is home to many species of fish, birds, and other animals. Willy has arranged for a swamp tour. Everyone climbs aboard a boat. They enjoy the quiet beauty of cypress trees draped in Spanish moss.

The tour guide tells you that most of the state's crawfish harvest comes from this swamp. Roxanne isn't surprised. She sees crawfish crawling everywhere! Count the number of crawfish in the scene. Then head straight to the bottom of page 19 to catch your next clue.

How many crawfish did you count?

Fewer than 100 crawfish?
The clue words are THIRD LETTER.

Exactly 100 crawfish?
The clue words are THIRD VOWEL.

More than 100 crawfish?
The clue words are FOURTH LETTER.

Turn to page 29 and write the clue words
on the correct line.

Cajun Cuisine

The crew continues west along Interstate 10. Roxanne drives straight into the heart of Cajun Country. This part of Louisiana contains more people of Acadian, or Cajun, heritage than anywhere else in the world. Acadians are of French-Canadian descent. They developed their own culture, which is known for its lively music and spicy food.

Willy's stomach rumbles just thinking about food. In Lafayette, the crew stops at a Cajun restaurant. After placing their orders, Willy and Roxanne try their hands (and feet!) at the Cajun Two-Step. When all the orders are ready, the waiter must figure out who gets each dish. Help him get their order in order. Then check the bottom of page 21.

Redfish

Gumbo

Bisque

Clues

1. Robomouse's and Willy's dinners cost the same amount.

2. Squawker eats only vegetables.

3. Sue's dinner contains crawfish.

4. Willy ordered extra lemon with his meal.

MENU

Chicken and Sausage Jambalaya
Rich pilaf with rice, sausage, ham, chicken, and tomatoes **$10**

Seafood Gumbo
Spicy soup made with okra, peppers, crabs, shrimp, and crawfish **$10**

Crawfish Etouffé
Crawfish cooked with onions and tomatoes, served over rice ..**$10**

Crawfish Bisque
Light crawfish soup served over rice ..**$9**

Blackened Redfish
Zesty chargrilled redfish **$9**

Boiled Crabs
Fresh Louisiana crabs **$9**

Corn-on-the-Cob
A heaping plateful! **$4**

Bayou Ratatouille
Mix of okra, eggplant, zucchini, and other vegetables ..**$4**

balaya

Did you figure out what each crew member ordered for dinner? What did Roxanne order?

If it's the Seafood Gumbo,
cross off the square and the basin.

If it's the Crawfish Bisque,
cross off the forest and the oak.

If it's the Chicken and Sausage Jambalaya,
cross off the plantation and the capitol.

Now turn to page 30 and use this clue.

FLORIEN FLORA

After their meal, the crew is ready for a long, scenic drive. Roxanne heads west along Interstate 10. She turns right on Route 171 and drives north. The central part of the state is known as the "crossroads" of Louisiana. Roxanne stops in Florien. This town is home to Hodges Gardens, Park and Wilderness Area. With 4,700 acres, it is the largest privately owned horticultural park and wildlife refuge in the country. The garden was created on the site of an old stone quarry. Today, it is a peaceful spot for nature lovers.

The crew hikes past waterfalls, moss-covered rocks, and flowerbeds. While everyone stops to smell the flowers, use your Pelican State knowledge to fill in the "crossroads" crossword on page 23. After you finish, plant yourself on the bottom of the page.

Don't Forget Your Map!
All the information you need to answer these clues can be found on your map of Louisiana.

Across

4. Town near the intersection of I-55 and I-12
6. Louisiana's first permanent European settlement
7. Southeastern Louisiana town on Highway 90 with more vowels than consonants in its name
9. State that borders Louisiana to the west
10. Rainiest major city in the country
11. River that flows along the border of Louisiana and 9 Across
12. Town where the crew is right now
13. Mountain forming Louisiana's highest point

Down

1. Capital of the state
2. Large lake north of New Orleans
3. Louisiana's southern border: Gulf of _____
5. A Louisiana eastern border river
8. Third-largest city in the state
9. Spelled-out number of the interstate that connects Lafayette and Lake Charles
12. Louisiana population ranking of 10 Across

22

Did you fill in all the answers? Some of the squares in the grid are shaded. Write the letters from the shaded squares here:

_____ _____ _____ _____ _____ _____ _____ _____

Now unscramble them to spell one word in the name of a famous place on page 30.

_____ _____ _____ _____ _____ _____ _____ _____

Cross this landmark off your list.

See the Lights

The crew heads up Route 171 to the Shreveport–Bossier City area. These two cities grew up on opposite sides of the Red River. The gang splits up and spends the day at some of Shreveport's fascinating museums. Roxanne enjoys the Western paintings in the R.W. Norton Art Gallery. Sue and Squawker check out the Sci-Port Discovery Center, the state's only "hands-on" interactive science museum. Willy and Robomouse explore the Louisiana State Exhibit Museum, famous for its towering murals showing state history.

At dusk, everyone enjoys seeing the lights of the Texas Street Bridge. This bridge, which connects the two cities, is the country's largest neon-lit bridge. As Sue admires the bridge, she starts thinking about other things that might connect Shreveport and Bossier City. Help Sue come up with a list of words using only letters from the names of these two sister cities. Then connect with a clue at the bottom of page 25.

SHREVEPORT

BOSSIER CITY

SHREVEPORT–BOSSIER CITY

1. Molars and incisors   __ __ __ __ __ __

2. Word that shows action in a sentence   __ __ __ __

3. Saddle-wearing animal   __ __ __ __ __

4. Another word for *avenue*   __ __ __ __ __ __ __

5. Sound a snake makes   __ __ __ __ __

6. Person on TV who brings you the news   __ __ __ __ __ __ __ __ __

7. Playtime in school   __ __ __ __ __ __

8. A baseball player in the infield   __ __ __ __ __ __ __ __ __ __

9. Wooly farm animal   __ __ __ __ __

10. Opposite of *brother*   __ __ __ __ __ __

11. Large boat   __ __ __ __

12. A crowing farm animal   __ __ __ __ __ __ __

Did you fill in all the answers? Some of the letters are circled. Write those letters, in order from *bottom* to *top*, in the spaces below.

Turn to page 30 and cross off

__ __ __ __   __ __ __ __   __ __ __ __ __ .

This is Louisiana's state beverage.

orange juice 3 →
milk 2

The first letters of each of the states that border Louisiana can spell this word.

← MAT 4

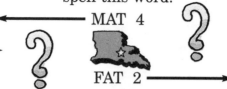

FAT 2 →

This was discovered near Jennings in 1901.

← coal 4
← oil 1

CLUE
Cross off the forest.

Get to the Point

Roxanne steers east along Interstate 20 and then north. Your final Louisiana stop is the Poverty Point State Commemorative Area, near the town of Epps. There are huge earthen mounds here, left by the earliest-known culture that lived in what is now Louisiana. This civilization arrived here about 3,000 years ago. By 700 B.C., it had vanished. The crew members head off to watch an archaeological dig. Meanwhile, you can dig up your last clue.

Place a marker, such as a penny or paper clip, on the space marked START. Choose the correct answer in that square. Then move forward or backward the correct number of spaces. Each time you land, you will have to choose another answer. In the end, you will land on one of the boxes marked CLUE. That has the final bit of information you need.

Don't Forget Your Map!
Your Louisiana map has all the answers you need.

New Orleans held its first Mardi Gras in this year.

1827 6
1819 6

CLUE
Cross off the square.

Louisiana's first world's fair took place in this year.

← 1984 3
1884 3 →

The state insect is *not* this.

honeybee 6 —
← ladybug 7

CLUE
Cut the capitol.

The town of Rayne has a large population of this type of frog.

bullfrog 3 →
← tree frog 4

CLUE
Trim the oak.

This is Louisiana's sixth-largest city.

↑

Lake Charles 2
Kenner 6

↓

This is Louisiana's state dog.

↑   ↑

Catahoula leopard dog 1
Bayou bloodhound 2

Did you land on a clue?
Turn to page 30 and use it to cross off one final Louisiana landmark.

CLUE
Purge the plantation.

The world's longest over-water bridge spans this lake.

← Grand 1
← Pontchartrain 2

CLUE
Banish the basin.

27

Who?

Which famous Louisianan will enter the Which Way Hall of Fame? To find out, solve the puzzles on pages 2 through 11. Each puzzle will help you eliminate one person from this list. When there is only one person left, you will have your answer.

Louis "Satchmo" Armstrong
Trumpet player, singer, and bandleader from New Orleans who became a world-famous jazz musician

Truman Capote
Author, born in New Orleans, whose works include *Breakfast at Tiffany's*, as well as many stories set in the South

Michael DeBakey
Heart surgeon who invented the first successful "assisting heart," a mechanical pump that helps hearts to work

Lillian Hellman
Playwright and author whose award-winning plays speak strongly against selfishness and injustice

Evelyn Ashford
Track star from Shreveport who competed in four Olympics, winning one silver and four gold medals

"Pistol" Pete Maravich
College basketball legend at Louisiana State University and member of the Basketball Hall of Fame

The person going into the Hall of Fame is:

What?

One item from Louisiana has been chosen to be displayed in the Which Way Museum. To find out what it is, solve the puzzles on pages 12 through 19. Each puzzle will give you a clue to write on a line below. When put together, the four clues will tell you what to do.

Plantation Sensations (pages 12-13)

_____

It's a Shore Thing (pages 14-15)

_____

Louisiana Language (pages 16-17)

_____

Swamped! (pages 18-19)

_____

Now write the circled letters, in the order you circled them, in the box below.

The item that will go into the Which Way Museum is:

___ _____ _____ _____

_____ _____ _____

Where?

One landmark from Louisiana is to be featured in the Which Way Supermax Movie. To find out where the Which Way cameras are going, solve the puzzles on pages 20 through 27. Each puzzle will help you cross off one or more of the famous places below. When you finish, the remaining landmark will be the answer.

Kisatchie National Forest
Louisiana's only national forest and a popular place for hiking, camping, and canoeing

Evangeline Oak
Tree from Henry Wadsworth Longfellow's famous epic poem "Evangeline" and a symbol of Acadiana

Jackson Square
Beautiful public plaza in the heart of New Orleans's French Quarter

New State Capitol Building
Thirty-four-story art deco building and the nation's tallest state capitol

Oakley Plantation
Site where John James Audubon painted many of the illustrations for his book *Birds of America*

Atchafalaya Basin
More than 800,000 acres of swampland that make up America's largest undeveloped wetlands

The famous place is:

All the answers for your
Which Way adventure
are on the next two
pages. Do not go

unless you need help
with a puzzle. If you
don't need help,

before you look at
the answers.

You can use the rest of
this page to work out
your puzzles. If you need
a little extra space,

your pencil here. After
you're done, make a

back to the page you
were working on.

ANSWERS

Pages 2-3: "Easy" Does It
The collected letters spell HOOP STAR.
Eliminate basketball great Pete Maravich
on page 28.

Pages 4-5: Carnival Code

THE GOLD MEDALIST

CAN GO.

On page 28, cross out Olympic track star
Evelyn Ashford.

Pages 6-7: All That Jazz

1. F A T   T U E S D A Y
   $\underset{1}{}$ $\underset{2}{}$

2. S P A N I S H   M O S S
   $\underset{3}{}$ $\underset{4}{}$ $\underset{5}{}$

3. N E W   O R L E A N S
   $\underset{6}{}$ $\underset{7}{}$

4. A C A D I A N S
   $\underset{8}{}$ $\underset{9}{}$

5. G R E A T   R I V E R   R O A D
   $\underset{10}{}$ $\underset{11}{}$ $\underset{12}{}$

6. A M E R I C A N   R O S E
   $\underset{13}{}$ $\underset{14}{}$

   S O C I E T Y
   $\underset{15}{}$

O N   P A G E   T W E N T Y - E I G H T,
$\underset{5}{}\underset{7}{}$ $\underset{3}{}\underset{12}{}\underset{10}{}\underset{13}{}$ $\underset{2}{}\underset{6}{}\underset{13}{}$ $\underset{7}{}\underset{2}{}\underset{15}{}\underset{13}{}\underset{9}{}\underset{10}{}\underset{4}{}\underset{2}{}$

   C R O S S   O F F   C A P O T E.
   $\underset{8}{}\underset{11}{}\underset{5}{}\underset{14}{}\underset{14}{}$ $\underset{5}{}\underset{1}{}\underset{1}{}$ $\underset{8}{}\underset{12}{}\underset{3}{}\underset{5}{}\underset{2}{}\underset{13}{}$

This eliminates author Truman Capote.

Pages 8-9: Terrace Twists

The moon and drum are each hidden twice.
Their first letters, **M** and **D**, are the initials
of **M**ichael **D**eBakey. Cross him off the list
on page 28.

Pages 10-11: Square Route
The collected letters are
Q, M, B, Z, X, S, J, H, I, and U.
The letters that come before each of these in
the alphabet spell PLAYWRIGHT. Cross off
playwright Lillian Hellman on page 28.

Pages 12-13: Plantation Sensations

```
M W E G N A L R A P R G
O A K L A W N M A N O R
U C G E F R O G M O R E
N I U N T E U T M H E E
T H E C O T T A G E G N
H E W O Z L D P L S A W
O O R E D E I L S O C O
P S T A W R T A T R O O
E D O O W E H T Y L B D
K A O E V I L A W E I T
H D N O M R O C T M H E
O C S I C N A R F N A S
```

The leftover letters spell WRITE THE
WORDS "START WITH THE." Write these
words on the correct line on page 29.

Pages 14-15: It's a Shore Thing
1. **t** 2. **h** 3. **i** 4. **r** 5. **d** 6. **a** 7. **a** 8. **n** 9. **d**
The clue words are THIRD "A" AND. Write
these words on the line on page 29.

Pages 16-17: Louisiana Language
Four of Squawker's statements (numbers 3,
5, 8, and 9) are incorrect. Write CIRCLE
EVERY on the correct line on page 29.